AF575526

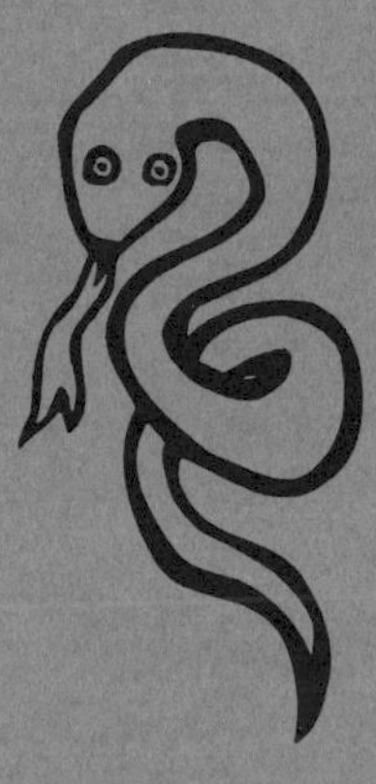

MEMORIES THAT SMELL LIKE GASOLINE

DAVID WOJNAROWICZ

MEMORIES THAT SMELL LIKE GASOLINE

DAVID WOJNAROWICZ

Foreword by
Ocean Vuong

A Note from the Editor
by Amy Scholder

NIGHTBOAT BOOKS
NEW YORK

Second Printing, 2026

Printed in Lithuania

Cover image: *Fuck You Faggot Fucker*
by David Wojnarowicz, 1984.

Nightboat Books would like to thank P.P.O.W. for their
assistance during the production of this book.

ISBN: 978-1-64362-271-2

Design and typesetting by Rissa Hochberger
Typeset in Resonanz B and Rockwell

Cataloging-in-publication data is available
from the Library of Congress

Nightboat Books
New York

www.nightboat.org

CONTENTS

A NOTE FROM THE EDITOR

When I was getting the first edition of *Memories That Smell Like Gasoline* ready for press in 1992, David was dying. It was our first and last book to prepare together. The other books by David that I published were posthumous. We decided to work on this one first because it felt so close to the reckonings we were having at the time. How memory has a smell and touch and feel. How it seems to change our DNA. How memorializing in words and pictures can find new meaning, keep something alive. Maybe.

I was living in San Francisco. My friend Rex Ray introduced me to Anne MacDonald, a curator and art collector who wanted to publish an imprint of books featuring contemporary art and writing. She hired me to be the editor. *Memories* was our first book in the series. The second book featured drawings by Nayland Blake and writings by Dennis Cooper.

David was living in a loft above the Village East movie theater on Second Avenue and 12th Street. It had been Peter Hujar's last apartment. Anita Vitale was there when USPS delivered the finished book from the printer to David's address. She was the best friend of Tom Rauffenbart, David's lover; he also had AIDS. David was bedridden by then. She opened the package and showed him the book. He wasn't speaking much at that point but communicated with his eyes as they went through the book together. When they got to the end, he wanted her to read aloud: "I am waving my hands. I am disappearing. I am disappearing but not fast enough." And then he said, Ah. And closed his eyes.

I was so relieved to hear that he got to see it. But I wondered, does a book really matter when you're at the end of a life cut short at the age of thirty-seven. Do you think, well, at least this will remain. I don't know how David really felt in that moment, but I do know that he loved books and had wanted to be a published author since he was an adolescent. So maybe this book mattered to him. I've learned since then that it has mattered to many other people.

Just three years after that summer when the book came out and David died, a treatment for HIV/AIDS hit the market; it would keep people who had access to it alive. Tom, who thought he was going to die soon after David, was on a clinical trial for this treatment in 1994. He lived to be seventy-four years old.

A few years after another pandemic, on September 14, 2024, I sat among a few hundred people in an AIDS memorial park in the West Village to celebrate what would have been David's 70th birthday. It was a beautiful event created by Anita, now the executor of David's estate. I was joined by Nayland, performer John Kelly, Karen Rinaldi (editor of *Close to the Knives*), and a long list of artists and writers, friends and fans of David's who read aloud from *The Waterfront Journals*, which I published in 1996. It was incredibly moving to hear these readings in a public square on this occasion. Afterwards, at dusk, a lot of us walked over to the Hudson River, to another AIDS memorial.

Unbeknownst to me, Anita had brought some of David's remains (he had been cremated), which Tom had never scattered. She thought it might be a good moment to let them go, in queer community, with so many people who loved David.

Anita took out a few ziplock bags from her purse. She had mixed in some of Tom, too. Why not. At first, I recoiled. It was hard to feel so emotional in front of all these people—many friends and acquaintances but even more strangers. Soon though, surrounded by young people who never knew David, I became overwhelmed by other feelings. Of their love for his work, for his legacy. It seemed to me that they wanted to experience this visceral, vertiginous act of touching him—what remains— and let the ashes go into the air, hopefully into the river. Of course the wind had different ideas.

The first story in *Memories*, "Into the Drift and Sway," is accompanied by watercolors that David made from memory after spending time at a porn theater. They form a diary of desire. Of memory and the ways we keep pleasure alive by imagining. That practice of David's inspires me to do this work year after year.

I'm so grateful to Stephen Motika, Lindsey Boldt, and Rissa Hochberger at Nightboat for rescuing this book from obscurity. To Isaac Alpert, Wendy Olsoff, and Penny Pilkington at PPOW for providing the artwork. And to Anita Vitale and the David Wojnarowicz Foundation for bringing forward David's legacy so thoughtfully and with love.

Amy Scholder
Los Angeles
December 18, 2024

DAVID WOJNAROWICZ'S RADICAL REFUSAL OF SHAME

I remember picking up a copy of *Close to the Knives* at the Housing Works Bookstore in Soho and reading the first few pages. Without knowing it, I had slid to the floor, my back pressed against a wall, breathing fast, my mind clicking in recognition of a voice I had sought for so long but had not had the language to name nor the compass to find. I was caught and pulled by the rage, wonder, sexiness, and, most vital to David's work, an ambivalent yet tender regard for lived experience—his voice, while inflected with pain and frustration, never forsakes the central desire to celebrate the act of living.

While *Close to the Knives* has an epic, polyphonic sweep that spans myriad swaths of David's life, *Memories That Smell Like Gasoline* is a quieter book, whose tone also signals its subversive power. Written in a diaristic voice one might use while catching up with a group of intimate friends gathered in an apartment living room: "All I remember is a beautiful view and my overwhelming urge to puke." The voice feels more communal, full of recounts and revisions, less lyrical and more crystalline. Vulnerable for being pared back, the sentences gain the bold simplicity of reportage, a precursor to the hybrid works of Maggie Nelson, Sam Ace, or Pamela Sneed.

"It is not just that violence fades into sweetness; it's looking at the flesh of the body and recognizing that it is a restraint that keeps the blood inside the form." This quote from the original 1992 edition of *Memories That Smell Like Gasoline,* published just two months after David's death at age thirty-seven from AIDS-related illness, serves as a thesis for much of Wojnarowicz's interdisciplinary work: the reality of the physical realm—the body, its hungers, pleasures, and failures—against the wish for art to ameliorate the material borders that often deny the artist's transcendence. In other words, the impossibility of radical transformation without destruction. To feel anything at all, the flesh must be obedient to the laws of blood and gravity. In this way, reading this collection—which veers between poetry, memoir, missives from abject yet necessary underbellies, and testimony from a salvaged youth—one gets the sense that the words keep trying to breach the medium of writing itself, as if the alphabet, given to us from a calcified system invented long before we arrived, is not enough, was never enough. "I am signaling that the volume of all this is too high…" David writes. "I am waving my hands. I am disappearing. I am disappearing but not fast enough."

David's work has inspired generations of Queer writers, myself included, since his untimely passing. Written in an era where our forerunners were lost too soon from the AIDS epidemic, when Reagan-era Christian conservatism was at its hysterical peak, when our voices were few and far between, David's work feels like a scream that echoes through the years—finding us now in a different yet not-too-changed socio-political hellscape. Inside the intimate encounters and experiences David animates, both with friends and strangers, there is never any judgment, even of the most fraught scenes. Getting a blow job in a theater while also getting your wallet stolen and staying to see the act through because that's where you've put yourself, what you've chosen, because, "We both understood each other," recentered crucial agency in an era when the Queer body was seen, even among community members, like something slipping out to sea.

Heteronormative readings of precarious Queer experiences, especially of casual encounters among gay men, have often been reduced to "trauma" or critically pigeon-holed as "trauma porn." Wojnarowicz reminds us, however, that trauma, clinically, is what's *felt* by an individual—not the action itself. Which is not to say that *Memories* is removed from the unsettling, gutting, and dangerous themes present in much of David's other work, but rather that not all violence becomes trauma in all nervous systems. Automatically pathologizing Queer experiences as trauma is mimetic of the historical treatment of Queer desire as error, failure, doomed and depraved, stripping the Queer body of the agency to define its own phenomenological reality. This is why Wojnarowicz's ambivalence, his refusal to shame and judge Queer experiences, while absolutely condemning the judgment of the state, feels so powerful to me today. Because despite feeling "like a ticking time bomb," as David writes, "we understand each other." What a nearly impossible gift then: to be understood, to be legible while also resisting definition, and to do so across time, long after the body dissolves, its borders erased. And the voice "shouting my invisible words," now preserved here by the labor of Queer archival salvage, is finally heard.

And it's heard by us.

Ocean Vuong
November 2024

MEMORIES THAT SMELL LIKE GASOLINE

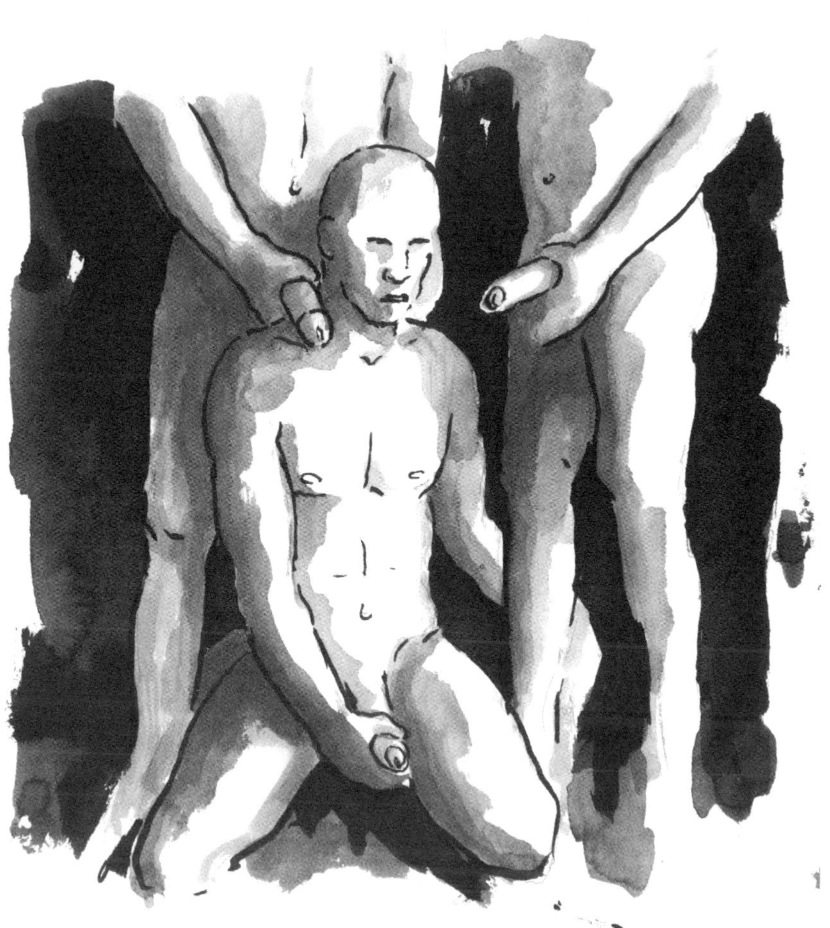

INTO THE DRIFT AND SWAY

Sometimes it gets dark in here behind these eyes I feel like the physical equivalent of a scream. The highway at night in the headlights of this speeding car speeding is the only motion that lets the heart unravel and in the wind of the road the two story framed houses appear one after the other like some cinematic stage set, houses on both sides of my face unravelling towards me and the trees casting

shadows like fallen x-rays into the sides
of the white clapboard and occasionally
some yard dog hooting a silent fear noise
it's lost in the rush of everything; and once
before when I felt this way I screamed loud
and long and hated the sound of my own
voice and so haven't ever tried it again. I
hate highways but love speeding and I can
only think of men's bodies and the drift and
sway of my own if sex was a dance I'd do a
crawl for that body I saw this afternoon the
guy stepping out from the cab of his truck
in the parking lot of the bus stop he looked
kinda canadian and in a sexy collared shirt
and tight faded jeans and thick leather belt
and boots and a crease in the front of his
pants that let his dick rest lazy and calm
and forearms I'd want under my tongue
and after the turn on the bridge when I'd
swung back going north stopped at a rest
stop and a truck pulled in I walked past

it a little later and a ruby red light flicked on and a silhouette of a man in worker's pants stepped out swinging from the bar next to the outside rear view mirror and walked past me in a blaze of car lights and entered the bathroom. I walked around for a while he never came back out finally I went in and bent slightly saw his legs beneath the frame of one of the stalls and took the one next to him pulled down my pants and sat on the cold toilet and looked down to my side and there was a puddle of water between the two stalls under the dividing panel and it reflected light from the overhead ceiling fixture and through its transparency was the squared outline of gray floor tiles and as I looked at it I realized that I could see the overhead-lit features of this truck driver and the pale wash of his eyes and jaw line and cheek bones and following the illuminated shoulders in

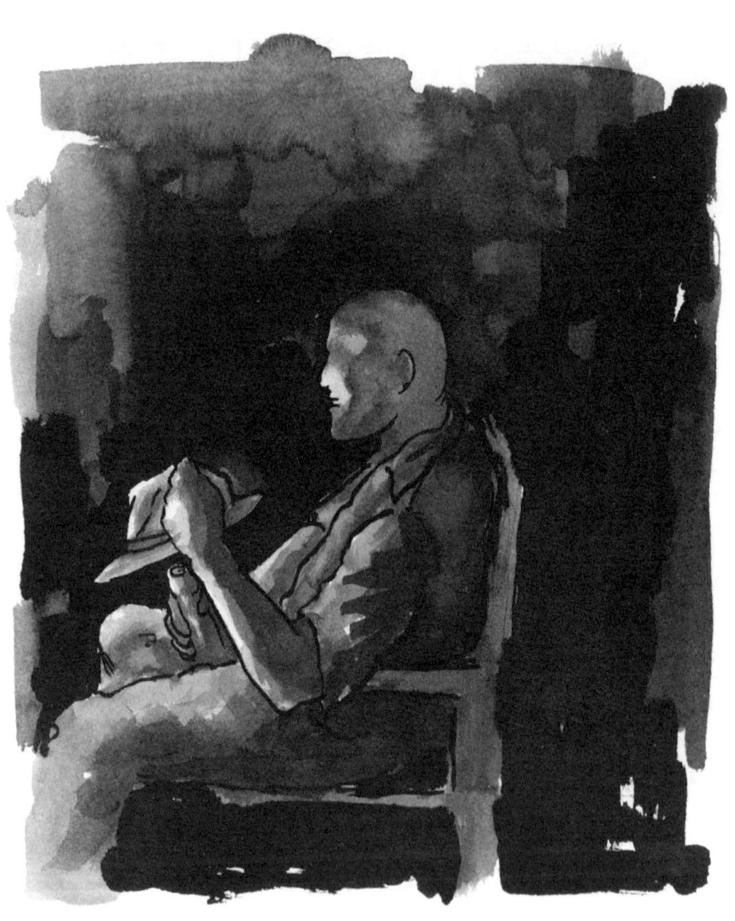

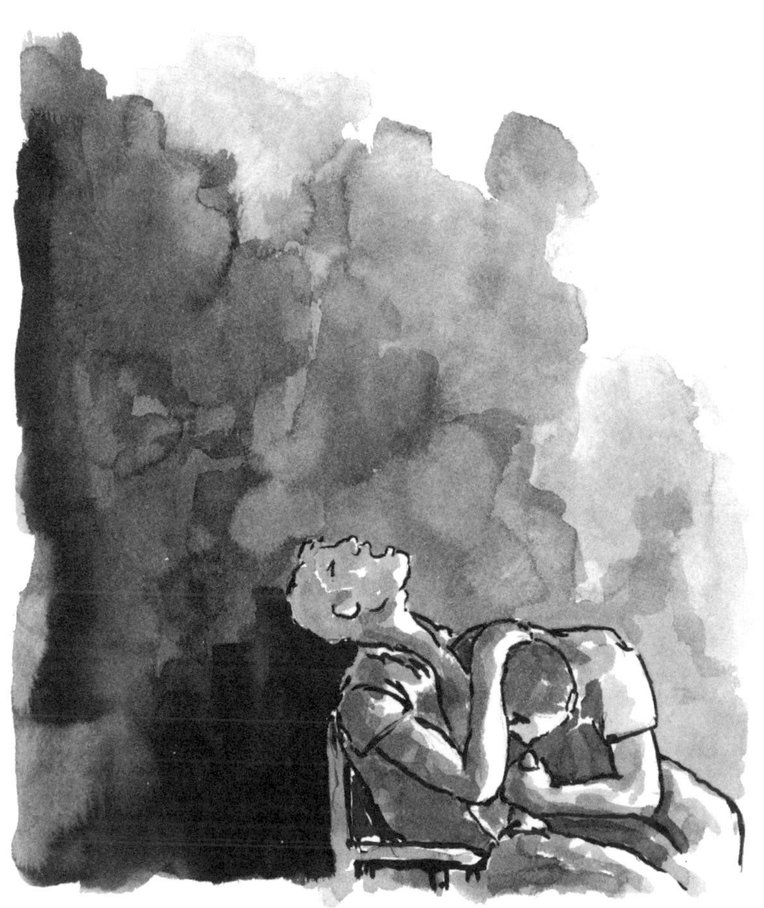

the surface of the puddle down his arms only one was illuminated and part of his chest pressing through the flimsy t-shirt and down his forearms and to his wrists and the puddle moved a bit breaking the image into wavy lines and pieces of light and when his face came back in focus and the water was still I held my breath so as not to disturb it I looked in the vicinity of his hands two hands lit from various angles pieces of fingers with cold white lights and parts of wrists and all of it wrapped around a silhouette of a hard dick which he waved back and forth in the reflection his image for a moment looked like it was floating upside down beneath the surface of the floor and I was therefore floating right side up and from his vantage point I was floating upside down and he right side up and up in the cab of his rig he pulled off his pants saying don't worry about the

cops they always check
the cars first and by
flashing their flashlights
through each one we got
plenty of time just to enjoy
it go ahead enjoy yourself
and putting his big hand
around the back of my
neck and pressing gently
till my face could make
out the outline of his
moving dick I could see
the dim hairs covering his
balls go ahead use your
tongue a lot and less teeth
that's it more tongue and
less teeth yeah where
I come from there's three
brothers who come over
my place when they can get
away they come over for

the night and they love it go
ahead that's right enjoy
it enjoy yourself. His fingers and face scattered into shards of light.

MEMORIES THAT SMELL LIKE GASOLINE

It's that face. I knew I'd seen it before. I was standing in the lobby of a movie theater surrounded by crowds of people waiting to enter the auditorium to watch a film about a bunch of teenagers and a dead body and codes of teenage silence. It was the end of the previous show and the doors flung open and hundreds of people were pouring out towards the exits. Suddenly that face. It was one anonymous face in the crowd that tripped the switch in the back of my head. I froze and the face became magnified. It expanded in size until it was five feet tall and disembodied and floating in the darkness of the open doors. I guess he froze too. He was a pale gray color with fastidiously combed hair plastered down around the skull. Thin lips, bloodless and tight. His eyes were colorless and they widened for a moment. We both stood there trying to uncoil each other's private histories and solve the dislocation of familiarity. I had been drugged, tossed out a second story window, strangled, smacked in the head with a slab of marble, almost stabbed four times, punched in the face at least seventeen times, beat about my body too many times to recount, almost completely suffocated, and woken up once tied to a hotel bed with my head over the side all the blood rushed down into it making it feel like it was going to explode, all this before I turned fifteen. I chalked it up to adventure or the risks of being a kid prostitute in new york city. At that point in my life dying didn't mean anything to me other than a big drag. I had mixed feelings about death. When I was trying to get enough money to eat or find a place to sleep for the night, death actually seemed attractive, an alternative. I would go without changing my clothes or bathing for months at a time. I could see my reflection in the legs of my pants if I bent close to them. Periodically if I had a surplus of money from spreading my legs in seven dollar hotels on Eighth Avenue I would walk into the Port Authority bus terminal and look at all the various names of towns painted on the glass windows of ticket booths. I'd choose one that suggested bodies of water and then buy a ticket, get on the bus and ride it for as long as it took till I spotted a lake or pond in the countryside. I'd then ask the bus driver to let me off, usually having to argue with him because it wasn't a scheduled stop. After the bus continued on its way I would walk across the field and into the water until I was up to my neck. I never bothered to take off my shoes or my clothes. I would float around for hours and then hike back to the road and hitch a ride to a bus-stop or all the way back into the city.

That face. When I noticed his suit and his hands, palms back and manicured nails, I remembered. Maybe it was the quality of light or lack of it in the lobby as the door swung open and people were exiting before the end of the film. Maybe it was the color of his flesh, the look of no oxygen, the look of anticipation or fear, the complexion of anticipation. I remember that night fifteen years earlier. I had spent the later part of the afternoon paddling around this small pond, pushing my face under water looking for signs of life. It was rapidly turning to dusk and I was wet and feeling cold. The town was too small to offer much evening traffic so it was hard to get a ride. I didn't really know where I was. I was gray inside my head and wishing that killing myself was an effortless act.

Those eyes, that face gray and floating disembodied in the dark of the open window. A small beat-up red pick-up truck coasted to a stop along the side of the road. He was waving me into the truck. I remember thinking his skin was fake, like a semi-translucent latex. I asked him how far he was going. Oh, a ways. Thin tight voice layered with a friendliness I couldn't hook into. We drove for a while in silence and I looked out the side window at all the illuminated houses and occasional glimpses of people in driveways, interacting with each other. A stray dog running along the highway in a small panic. He said he worked for a bank in the city. That depressed me for some reason, maybe the formality of it that translated into an image of years and years of writing in ledgers and stale cups of coffee and dealing with people in need. At some point he had his dick out and stared out through the windshield at the beacons of light illuminating the dark roadway. He steered with one hand and jerked with the other. I was leaning against the door and didn't answer when he murmured something about this place he knew where we could go. After a while he made a left turn down a gravel and dirt road winding up through a forest over small hills. I remember moths and bugs diving into the headlights, a small wooden sign with a boy scout symbol on it, and then some scattered cabins. The sound of lake water in the near distance.

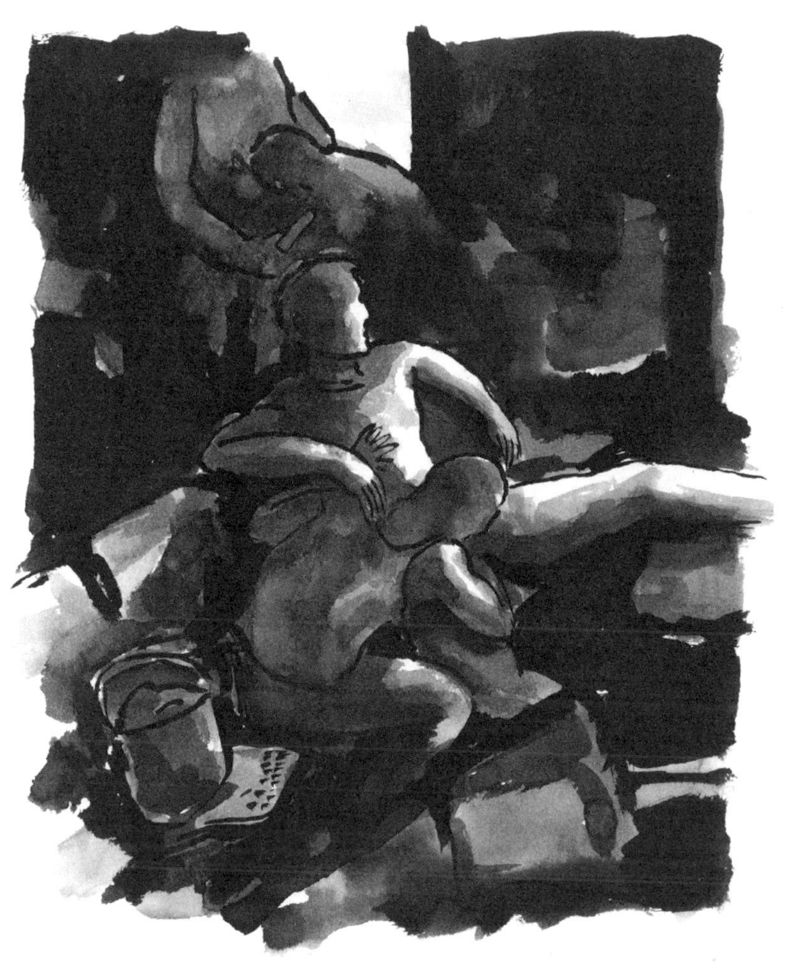

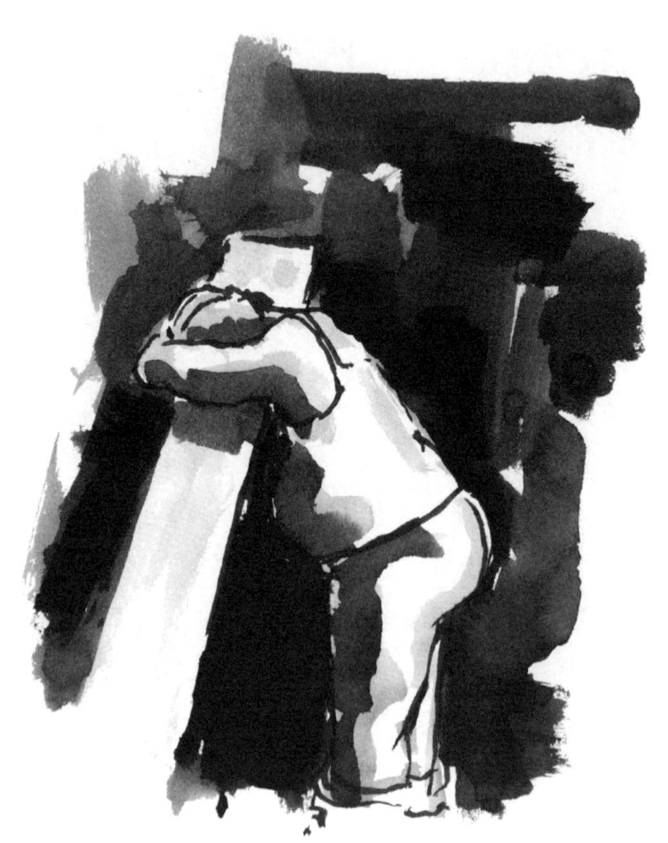

He got out of the driver's seat and pulled open the passenger door I was seated behind. Squat down and make it squirt. I didn't move. He had shut the engine and the headlights off. Get out. I felt suddenly much more tired than I ever remember feeling. I swung my legs out from the seat and stood in front of him with my hands in my pockets. A wind was coming up and it was starting to bring with it a light rain. He took me by the arm and led me to the back of the truck and turned a metal latch and swung up the back door of the camper. One of his hands floated up to my face and then encircled the back of my neck and I realized I was being propelled forward towards the black interior of the camper. I crawled obediently inside, it was loaded with blankets and sleeping bags and boxes of indecipherable stuff. It was kind of moist and smelled like earth and grease. He climbed in behind me and pulled the door shut. Everything was reduced to smells and the sound of trees and the squeak of his shoes against the metal parts of the floor. I lay down and curled up on a mass of smelly cloth. I could see his silhouette half-rise before me, blocking out the minimal light and then dropping to my side. The sound of a zipper opening. His hand on my neck again. Pulling. I want to go home, I said. What are you talking about? I realized his head was further back in the truck than I had thought. I couldn't see anything. The rain was coming down hard; sheets of water making the dimness more dark. I don't know, I said, wondering where I would go even if I got out of the truck without him stopping me. You like it in your ass? No. Good, he said and then hit me. Very hard.

I'm blind to the world and he's turning me over and over and over. Where am I? In a muddy field in the back of a stranger's truck and the truck is backed up to a fence and the stranger has put his full weight on my back and I feel like I'm in motion like something flung out of a giant sling shot. A pale length of rope hastily torn out of a wet cardboard box and wrapped around my hands pulled behind my back. I'm on my belly and if I yelled or hollered the only thing to hear me is the dead house miles back on the road dark and empty. Or the handful of rundown shuttered factories on the main road. He's pulling my hair, yanking my head back so his face appears upside down floating before mine and he's smiling. But the smile looks like a frown, it's upside down and he leans in and kisses both my eyes. The windows have fogged up and he opens one slightly and I can hear the occasional shine of an insect. He's slapping my bare butt and driving his tongue into my ear and running it down over the line of my neck and turning me over and over periodically. I'm overwhelmed by the smell of wet metal and the musky thickness of the cloth when my face is ground into a blanket or sleeping bag. What's he doing kneeling on my head, I ain't no doll with replaceable body parts. He's stuffing a rolled up blanket beneath my naked body forcing my ass up into the air. I can't feel my hands any more all the circulation is gone. Funny how everything all my life moved excruciatingly slow until this moment and now I'm just begging for it to stop. He giggles and disappears from the truck. I hear the sound of shoes on the grit and wetness of the road and the truck dips as he climbs back in. He lies on top of me. I'd feel

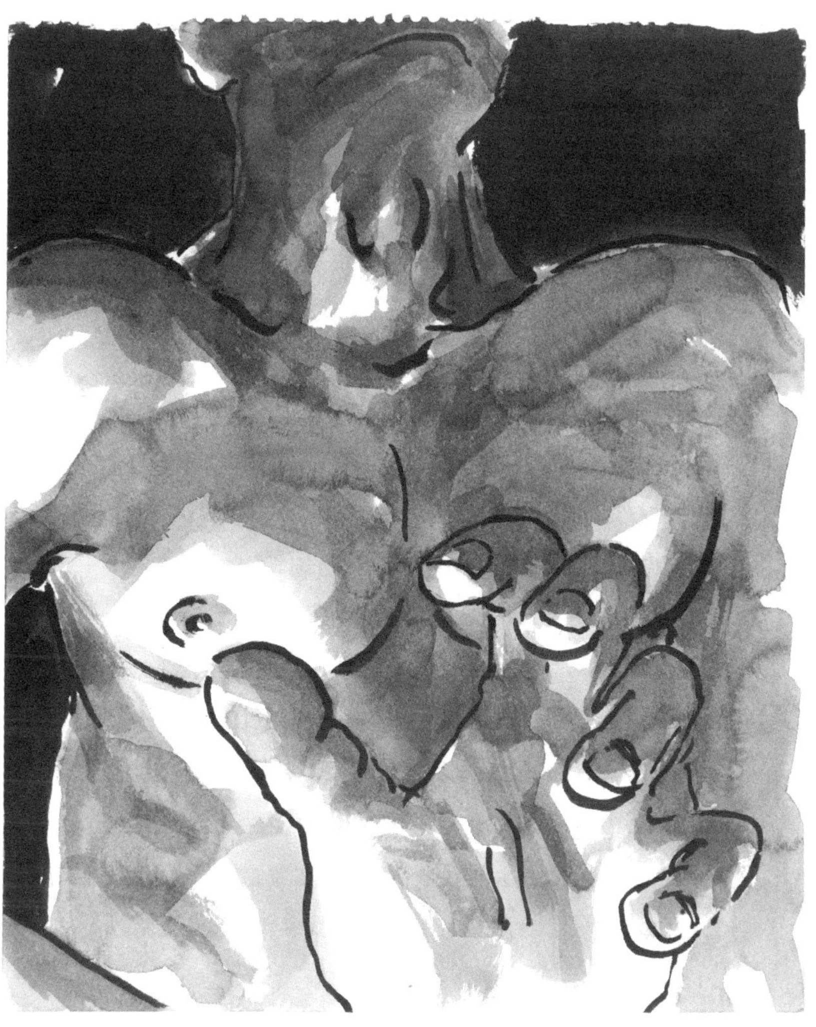

fucking cold but his body is generating intense heat. His shirt's off and his pants are down or gone. He starts slamming his body down on top of mine periodically his arm curving around my face. Lick that bicep. His arm pulls back, fingers shove something in my mouth; it's a wad of mud and sand. He treats me like he owns me. I'm stuck in a drift, lost, no hope, or anything familiar. Maybe now I'll get relief, maybe he'll crush my skull or strangle me. Suddenly I recall something from earlier when he loosened my belt and dragged my pants down to my calves and smacked me as hard as he could and it hurt so bad I tried to make it sexual I tried to imagine it was gentle or that he was somebody sexy or that I was a mile away walking in the opposite direction. Oh hit me I said trying to act like I was into it so maybe he'd get bored. Turning over and over and over what the fuck is he doing that for? He lunges and reaches far into the darkness of the truck and I hear a container of liquid, sounds like a metal container and liquid sounds the image of lighter fluid or gasoline went through my mind. Is this it? I could see the flames; I could see my body being turned over by campers looking like a side of beef left too long in the fire, black and charred with bones poking out of it. I felt the squirt of liquid all over my ass, a memory smell from childhood flooding the truck. Baby oil. I just want to die, I just want to die, I just want to die. If say it often enough will I lose my fear of his hands tightening around my throat? I'm sinking in dark pools of atmosphere and his palm is sliding around the small of my back, into the crack of my ass cheeks. Oh what a gift you're giving me, he mumbles. He grabs my tied arms pressing his full weight on them pinning my elbows at an outrageous angle to the cold metal floor and he shoves his dick into me. Ow. He's biting my cheek. Slap. Slap. Burying his face in my neck and biting again. I'm still sinking and his bites and slaps are so specific I think he hasn't lost control just four fingers in my mouth weight holding me down kissing my eyes breathing hard in my ear pumping like a machine. You like that steady rhythm? Uh.

In the codes that I carry in the sleepy part of my head, personal histories can turn on a dime and either rush away into disintegration or else turn and speed towards me looking to envelop. In the moment he was swept up in the crowd and moving across the lobby towards me I shrunk mentally and in size like a kid with no defenses not even my pocket knife. I wanted walls to suddenly and

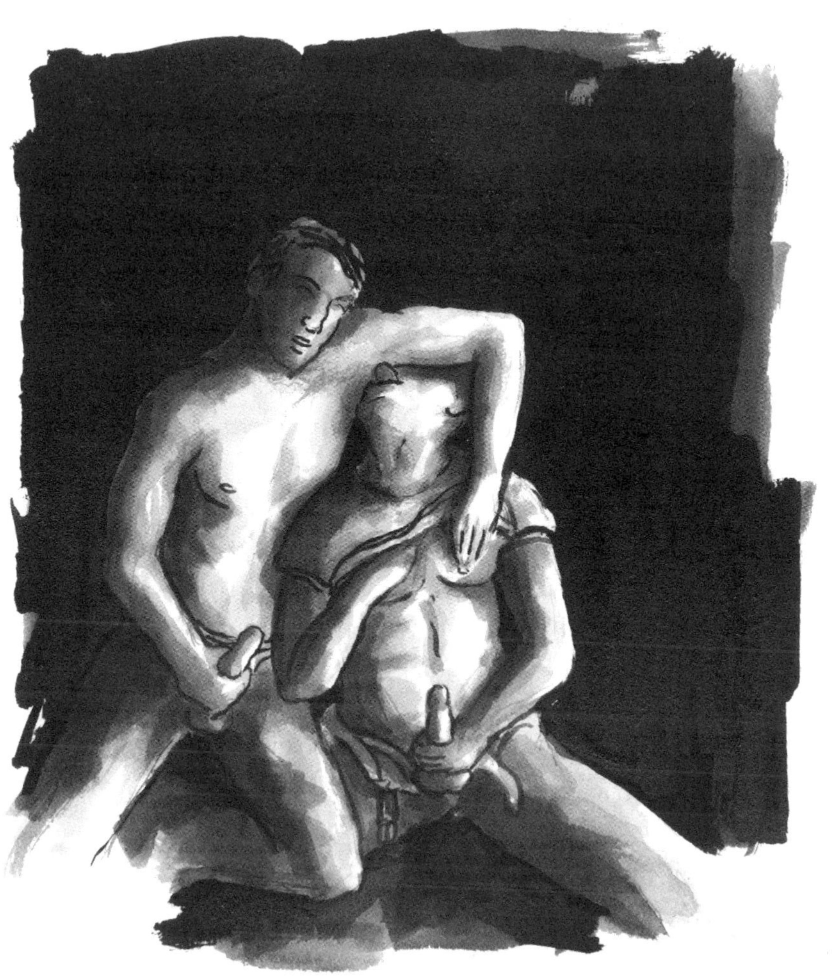

abruptly burst out of the floor and rise between us. I wanted dozens of walls made of reinforced concrete and steel to keep us separated, to keep his hands from touching me. But I knew he would smash through them like some kind of dream psycho. It was like he was bleeding me right there in the crowded room. All my history and language had suddenly been erased. I knew somewhere that I could finally beat him up but I was stuck looking at him through the eyes of a fifteen-year-old skull. I just kept thinking I wanted to kill his gaze. Something weird happened where I physically shrunk and I took the moment where he and I lost track of each other to duck down the staircase to the restrooms. I went into a stall and sat on the turned down toilet seat for a long time listening to the sounds of dozens of people coming in and out to piss. When

I finally went back upstairs he seemed gone. But I could still feel his gaze; it lingered like the stink after a bad fire.

DOING TIME IN A DISPOSABLE BODY

Just below Eighth Street I tipped into a greek diner and sat on a stool near the cash register. It was almost empty except for the cook, the counter man, and a woman who looked like she hadn't washed in a long time. She mumbled a lot and ran her fingers through her hair as the counter man worked on her trying to pick her up. Finally he brought me some coffee and the piece of pie I'd asked for then returned to the woman. Halfway through my meal the door swung open and this deaf mute walks in and leans against the counter a couple of seats from me. He uttered a series of squeaks and grunts and flashed me a smile. Something clicked in my head, I mean, he was intense and oddly sexy with a muscular body covered in scrapes and a few bruises. He looked like he just walked out of some waterfront in an old queer french novel. He managed to order a burger to go and as the counter man went in the back to place the order he leaned over the counter and lifted the plastic lid of the danish case and slipped one inside his filthy shirt. He winked at me as he speared a second danish and dropped it down his neckline, then he walked over and extended his hand and I shook it. Something was clicking somewhere. When I shook his hand he made an odd little gesture with his middle finger against my palm and winked again. There was an air of desperation and possible violence around him like a rank perfume. And that was what suddenly became sexy to me. I tried to understand this sensation, why the remote edge of violence attracts me to a guy. I associate with certain gestures or body language or scars or other physical characteristics an entire flood of memories and fictions and mythologies. It's something in the blue-ink tattoos or coal-scratched rubbings made in prison cells or in delinquent basement parties. Maybe it's the sense that he could easily and dispassionately murder some-one or rob a liquor store or a small roadside gas station or bang some salesman in the head at a highway rest stop and steal his automobile; it's something about the sense of violence carried as a distancing tool to break down the organized world. It's the weird freedom in his failure to recognize the manufactured code of rules. The violence that floats like static electricity that completely annihilates the possibility of future or security; I'm attracted to living like that, moment to moment, with very little piling up of information, breaking the windows of cause and response. Beyond all this it's also what happens when violence hangs above the road to the sexual act, that gets subverted within the series of small kissing motions at the base of my dick or across the underside of my balls. The sweetness of the sad lips of that criminal face lowering itself around my dick and the quiet sucking motion that I guide him into. It is not just that violence fades into sweetness; it's looking at the flesh of the body and recognizing that it is a restraint that keeps the blood inside the form; where the blood of the body creates a pressure so that it would spray out in every direction if it were not for the skin holding

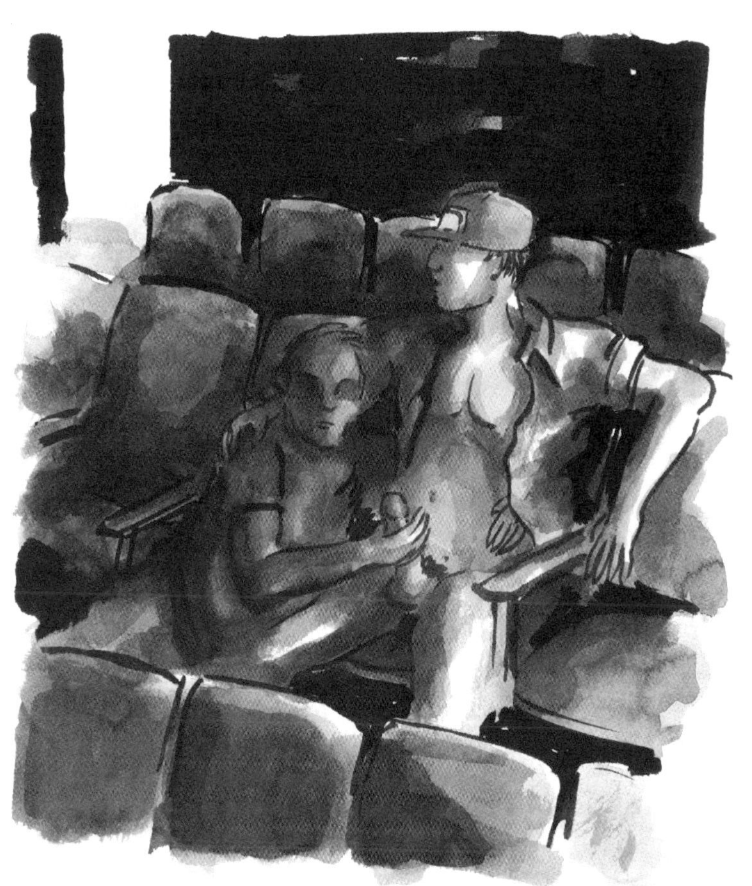

it back; it's sensing the history of that body and the temporariness of it all. I understand that his body and mind have no understanding of the proscriptions of this society's values; that time is lost to him except for progressions of gestures that attempt to satiate hungers of various sorts. When I engage with a guy like this I am laying open a trust, illusory or otherwise, that can strip open all the body's desires, and for a brief moment of living we let ourselves get lost.

He followed me across the street into the Sixth Avenue subway, down two flights of stairs, nobody around but one passenger running for a train down a faraway staircase in the gloom. I slowed up and was in between station platforms when he grabbed me and pulled me close. There was something silly about it but I didn't resist because it was hot too. He pulled open his pants revealing more scrapes on his muscular legs and his prick was growing hard and he formed the soundless words: I like you. His enormous hands pulled apart my shirt and slid around my chest and under my arms and pulled my shirt back over my shoulders, his grizzled face burrowing into my neck. The earth has a volume, my brain has a volume, and I can't turn it down; I can't shut it off, but it's moments like this that I sure know how to swim inside it. He's going into a slow motion crouch, his hands moving around rapidly like animated birds. As my dick is beginning to slide into his mouth I realize he's trying to pick my back pocket. I pulled his hands away and lifted them to my mouth where I sucked on his fingers. He looked up still blowing me trying to read my eyes like a bulletin. My eyes were blank. He slowly pulled his hands away from my mouth and eased them back towards my pockets. We both understood each other. I locked onto his hands again and threaded my fingers through his and made fists and started fucking his face more violently. I didn't know if he was armed and I was trying to figure out my exit. On the platform below I could hear my train approaching from the distance. It was almost painful the way he twisted his fingers till I let go and his hands insistently went to my pockets; he was starting to get rough. I leaned over and kissed the top of his head and thrust my knee forward sudden and sharp catching him in the chest, sending him backwards down a couple of stairs, that startled mouth gaping and those eyes opening wide, enough time to pull my pants closed and rush down the steps three at a time to the train whose doors had just begun to open. I hopped on with him behind me bellowing and the train doors

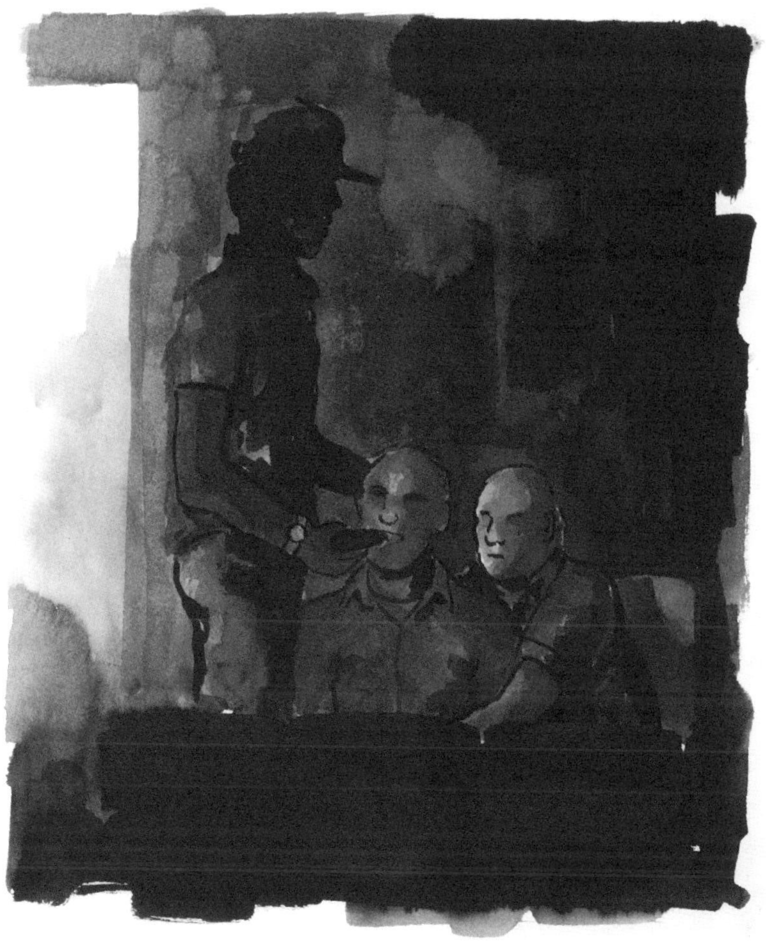

shut with him on the other side, fingers trying to press between to pull them apart, rage coloring his face. He never got in and I turned and slumped into a seat and realized the car was filled with sleeping winos. Christmas eve and I'm on a train full of drunks heading toward another future.

SPIRAL

1

Back near the monitor the blazing light of the hand jerking the hardened dick is creating a blind spot to the right of it in the room and I can just about make out some silhouetted shape of a guy in shorts and shirt opened, knowing this because as he moves from dick to dick his shirt floats like a curtain billowing into light and disappearing again and he's got a baseball cap on. I'm moving into this blind spot to watch and he's on his knees sucking some kid's prick. There's an old man in the darkest shadows his flesh is a bland color just a dead white, emptied of blood and he seems afraid of the light keeps shifting weight from one foot to the other in a squatting position at some point the sucking guy has his back to the old man and he's leaning over the ledge to get another guy's prick in his mouth and the old man takes a large hand and peels the guy's shorts down in a slow motion insistence and soon has his tongue planted firmly between the guy's cheeks. The guy starts rolling his ass in the air in circular motions and continues sucking the prick of the stranger before him. The old guy is lapping away like a puppy with a bowl of milk and I'm standing there in the darkness and there's a stream of water or something snaking across the floor and the pale glow of faces staring towards us

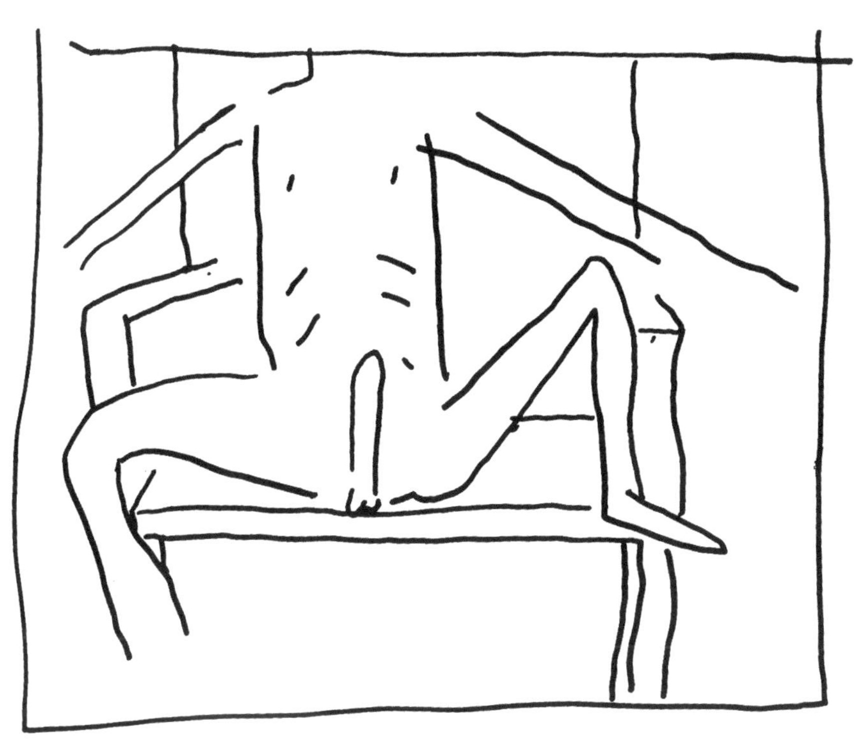

when I was 9 or 10 some guy picked me up in central park + took me home. He made a polaroid of me sitting in a chair. It didn't show my face so I let him keep it.

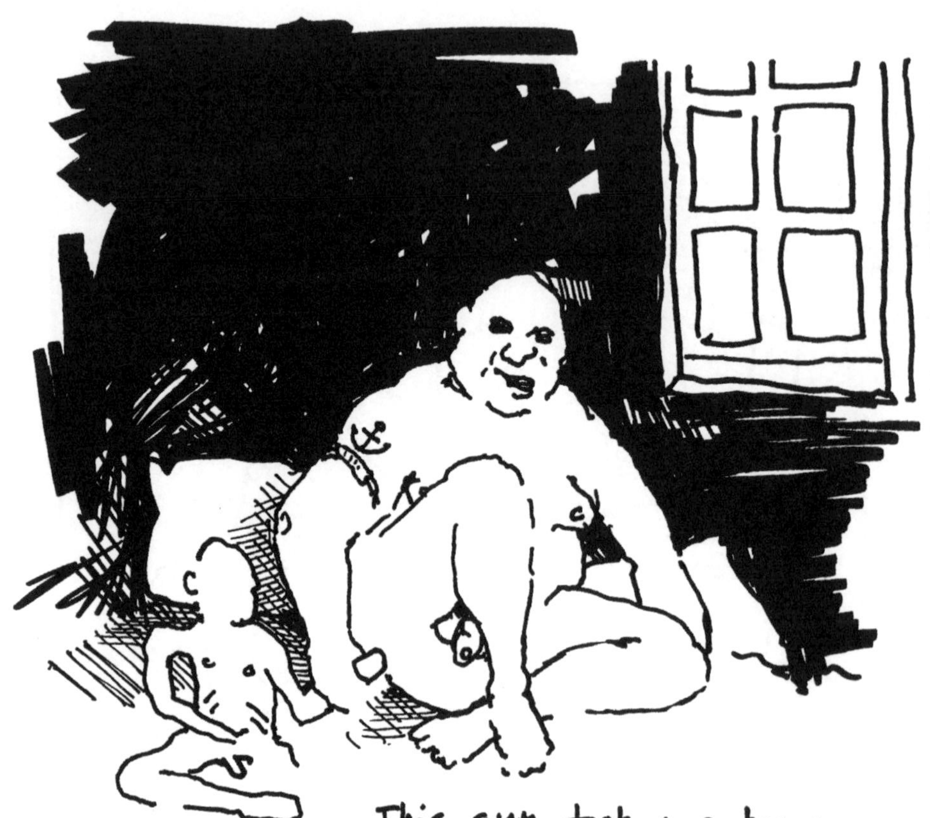

This guy took me home and at one point grabbed my arm and said make a fist. He suddenly pushed it against his butt. My hand disappeared. I was all shook up. Where did my hand go? I wondered.

at the monitor that I can only see sideways and on the angled screen is a pair of eyes looking dreamily up at the owner of a fat dick that's slowly sinking down his throat. A man enters the basement and walks over in my general direction momentarily blinded by the monitor and he runs into me before his eyes adjust, instead of backing up he reaches out and pulls me into a hug his arms muscled and hard and his embrace is squeezing air from my lungs. I rub my hands over the surface of his body his clothes and an almost indiscernible dampness to his shirt his body hard as wood his lips grazing my neck his hand pulling my head down so that he can softly bite the nape of my neck dragging his tongue around to my ear up and down the lines of my throat and my fingers are loosening his belt and my hands slip through his open zipper into all that warmth inside his underwear and down under his balls and his hand is on the back of my neck on my shoulders and he's pushing and I'm sinking down slow into a crouching position and from there slipping my hands beneath the edge of his white t-shirt and the t-shirt is tight and he's beginning to sweat his body generating intense heat and my mouth is opening and I'm licking under his balls the length and head of his dick is falling across the bridge of my nose resting against my eyelids and one of my hands swings up to wipe across my mouth to collect spit and then falls to my cock and I'm slicking it up with spit creating a random rhythm while licking at the base of his dick his hands are in my hair moving around cradling the base of my skull. As I stand back up I'm losing myself in the pale cool color of his flesh in the shadows and he takes my head in his

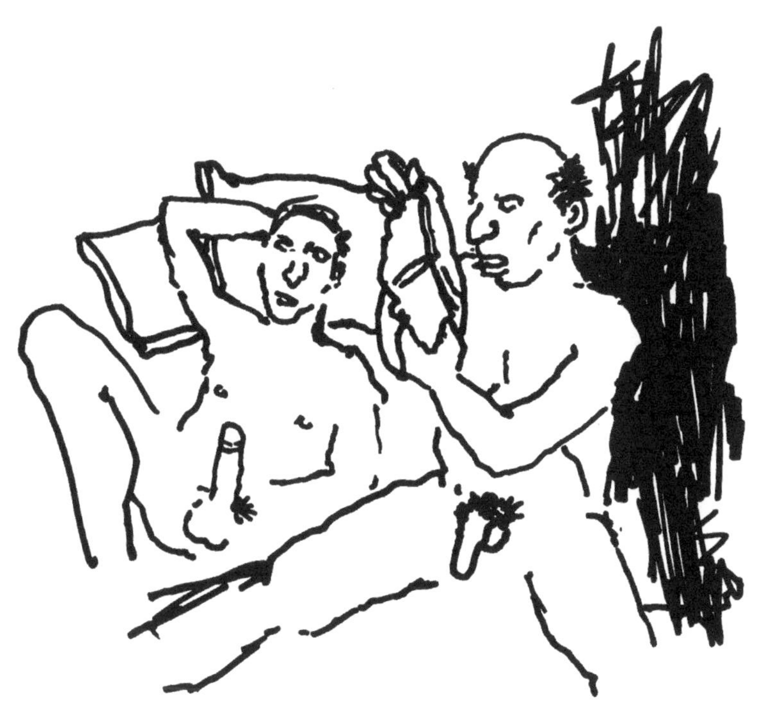

I Was ten years old. An old guy and his son picked me up and took me to a motel in midtown. He demanded that I give him my underwear to examine. what you lookin for I asked. Green spots. V.D. he said.

hands and pulls my face close to his gaze and I realize he's one of those guys that you know absolutely that if you'd met him twenty years earlier you both could have gone straight to heaven but now mortality has finally marked his face. He was really sexy though; he was like a vast swimming pool I wanted to dive right into.

2

All I can remember was the beautiful view and my overwhelming urge to puke. I was visiting my friend in the hospital and realizing he was lucky. Even though he was possibly going blind he did get the only bed in the room that had a window and a view. Sixteen floors up overlooking the southern skies as all the world spins into late evening. It was a beautiful distance to drift in but I still wanted to throw up. There among the red and yellow clouds drifting behind the silhouettes of the skyline was the overwhelming smell of human shit. It was the guy in the next bed; all afternoon he'd been making honking sounds like a suffocating goose. He was about ninety years old and I only got a glimpse of him and saw that they'd strapped an oxygen mask over his leathered face and when he screamed it sounded like a voice you'd hear over a contraption made of two tin cans and a piece of wire. Calling long distance trying to get the operator. Someone in charge. Someone in authority. Someone who could make it all stop with a pill, a knife, a needle, a word, a kiss, a smack, an embrace. Someone to step in and erase the sliding world of fact.

3

This kid walks into my sleep he's maybe seventeen years old stretches out on a table says he's not feeling well. He may be naked or else wearing no shirt his hands behind his head. I can see a swollen lump pushing under the skin of his armpit. I place my hands on his stomach and chest and try to explain to him that he needs to be looked at by a doctor. In the shadows of this room in the cool blue light the kid, a very beautiful boy, looks sad and shocked and closes his eyes like he doesn't want to know or like somehow he can shut it all out. Later some guy appears in the place. He has an odd look about his face. He tries to make it known that he knows me or someone close to me. He leans in close has flat dull eyes like blue silvery coins behind his

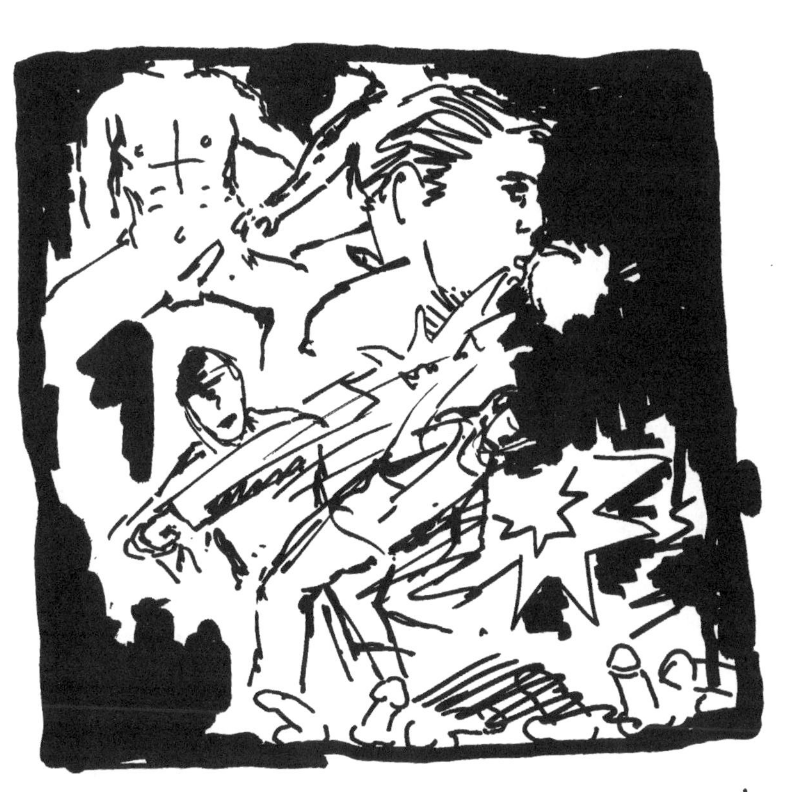

in this dream there was this young guy about 21 and he was aware that I wanted to kiss him and he demanded to fight. I found I had somehow learned all these great boxing moves - I beat him up just a little to get him to stop bothering me. I still wanted to kiss him.

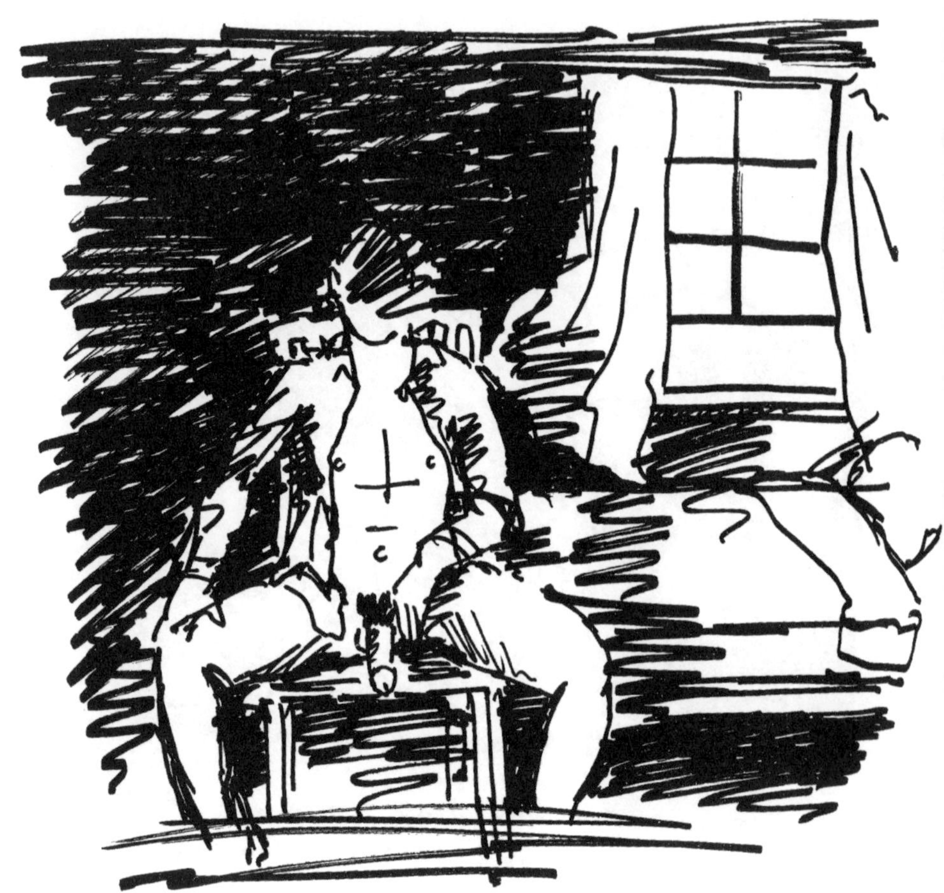

I was about 10 years old this guy took me to a hotel on 34 St and 8th avenue and sat in a chair with out his pants and asked me to blow him. he promised he wouldn't come in my mouth. I started sucking him and his face got red and he came in mymouth. I remember the wind in the curtains over the bed. I remember I wanted to kick his ass too.

irises. I think it is the face of death. I get agitated and disturbed and want to be left alone with the kid. Try to steer him away to some other location. He disappears for a moment and then reappears in the distance but far away isn't far enough. I turn and look at the kid on the table he looks about ten years old and water is pouring from his face.

4

Two blocks south there is a twenty story building with at least three hundred visible windows behind which are three hundred tiny blue television screens operating simultaneously. Most of them are tuned to the same stations you can watch the patterns of fluctuating light pop out like in codes. Must be the war news. Twenty seconds of slow motion video frames broadcasting old glory drifting by in the bony hands of white zombies, and half the population ship their children out on the next tanker or jet to kill and be killed. My friend on the bed never watches his tv. It hangs anchored to the wall above his bed extended over his face and on the end of a gray robotic-looking arm. If he bothered to watch the tv he would see large groups of kids in the saudi desert yakking about how they were going to march straight through to baghdad, find a telephone booth and call home to mom and dad. Then he'd see them writing out their wills on the customary government-supplied short forms. Or maybe he'd catch the video where the commanding instructor holds up a land mine the size of a frisbee and says, If you step on one of these there won't be nothing left of you to find . . . just red spray in the air. Or the fort dix drill sergeant out of view of the rolling cameras, When ya see those towel-heads . . .

But my friend is too weak to turn the channels on other people's deaths. There is also the question of dementia, an overload of the virus's activity in his brain short-circuiting the essentials and causing his brain to atrophy so that he ends up pissing into the telephone. He sees a visitor's face impaled with dozens of steel nails or crawling with flies and gets mildly concerned. Seeing dick cheney looming up on the television screen with that weird lust in his eyes and bits of brain matter in the cracks of his teeth might accidentally be diagnosed as dementia. I catch myself just as all this stomach acid floods up into my throat, run out to the hallway to the water fountain.

5

It's a dark and wet concrete bunker, a basement that runs under the building from front to back. There is one other concrete staircase that is sealed off at the top by a street grate and you can hear the feet of pedestrians and spare parts of conversations floating down into the gloom. At a mid-point in the room you can do a 360 degree slow turn and see everything; the shaky alcoves built of cheap plywood, a long waist-high cement ledge where twenty-three guys could sit shoulder to shoulder if forced to, the darkened ledge in the back half hidden by pipes and architectural supports, and the giant television set. It's one of the latest inventions from japan, the largest video monitor available and it is hooked into the wall, then further encased

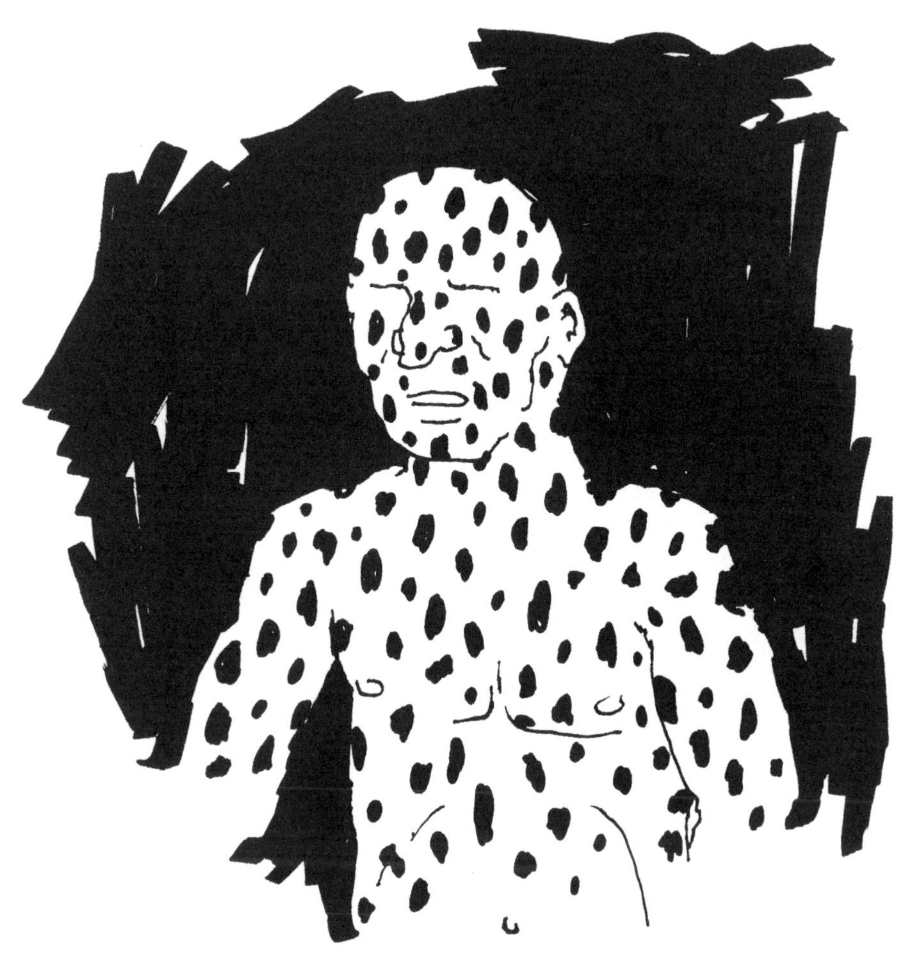

He burst into my home naked and covered in Kaposi threw me on the bed: "you would've thought I was sexy if you saw me before I got sick." I kissed him then pushed him off and ran from the apartment. Woke up.

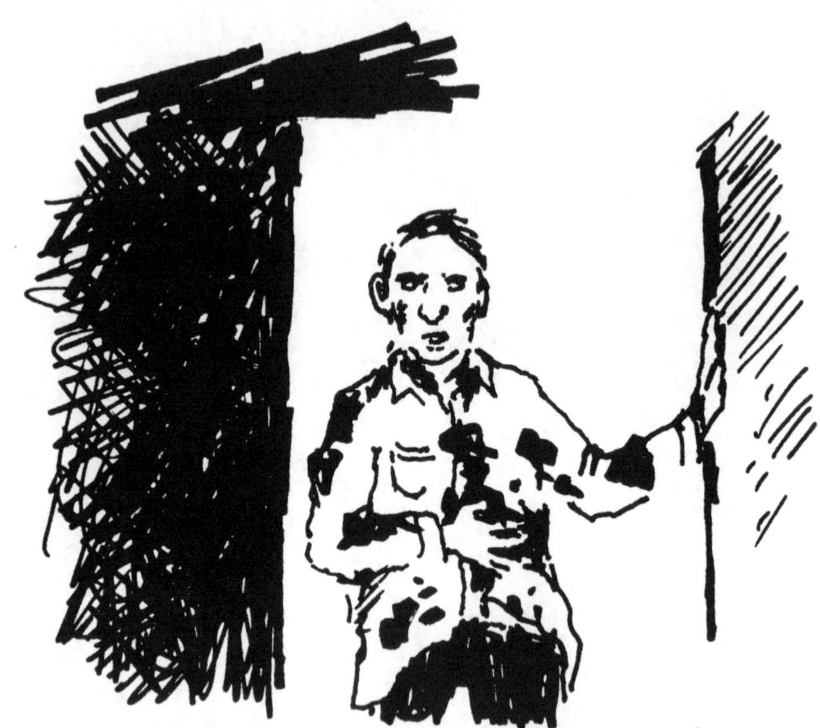

I was living in this cheap water front hotel. A young rich guy lived down the hall. He would always stay out late looking for hustlers on the waterfront. Late one night he appeared at my door covered in blood: "I made a mistake I think."

in a large sheet of plexiglass in order to prevent the hands of some bored queen from fucking with the dials and switching the sex scenes to Let's Make A Deal. The plexi is covered in scratches and hand prints and smudges and discolored streaks of body fluids. At the moment the images fed from a vhs machine upstairs are a bit on the blink. When the original film was transferred it was jumping the sprockets of the projector and now I'm watching images that fluctuate strobically up and down but only by a single centimeter. Each body or object or vista or close-up of eye, tongue, stiff dick and asshole is doubled and vibrating. Kind of pretty and psychedelic and no one is watching it anyway. There is a clump of three guys entwined on the long ledge. One of them is lying down leaning on one elbow with his head cradled in another guy's hand. The second guy is feeding the first guy his dick while a third guy is crouching down behind him pulling open the cheeks of his ass and licking his finger and poking at its bull's-eye. The shadows cast by their bodies cancel out the details necessary for making the vision interesting or decipherable beyond the basics. One of the guys, the one who looks like he's praying at an altar, turns and opens his mouth wide and gestures towards it. He nods at me but I turn away. He wouldn't understand. Too bad he can't see the virus in me, maybe it would rearrange something in him. It certainly did in me. When I found out I felt this abstract sensation, something like pulling off your skin and turning it inside out and then rearranging it so that when you pull it back on it feels like what it felt like before, only it isn't and only you know it. It's something almost imperceptible. I mean the first minute after being diagnosed you are forever separated from what you had come to view as your life or living, the world outside the eyes. The calendar tracings of biographical continuity get kind of screwed up. It's like watching a movie suddenly and abruptly going in reverse a thousand miles a minute, like the entire landscape and horizon is pulling away from you in reverse in order to spell out a psychic separation. Like I said, he wouldn't understand and besides his hunger is giant. I once came to this place fresh from visiting a friend in the hospital who was within a day or two of death and you wouldn't know there was an epidemic. At least forty people exploring every possible invention of sexual gesture and not a condom in sight. I had an idea that I would make a three minute super-8 film of my dying friend's face with all its lesions and sightlessness and then take a super-8 projector and hook it up with copper cables to a car battery slung in a bag over my shoulder and walk back in here and project the film onto the dark walls above their heads. I didn't want to ruin their evening, just wanted maybe to keep their temporary worlds from narrowing down too far.

6

The old guy is still honking away when I get back to the room. There are tiny colored lights wobbling through the red threads of dusk and I'm trying to concentrate on them in order to avoid bending over suddenly and emptying out. I've been trying to fight the urge to throw up for the last two weeks. At first I thought It was food poisoning but slowly realized it was civilization. Everything

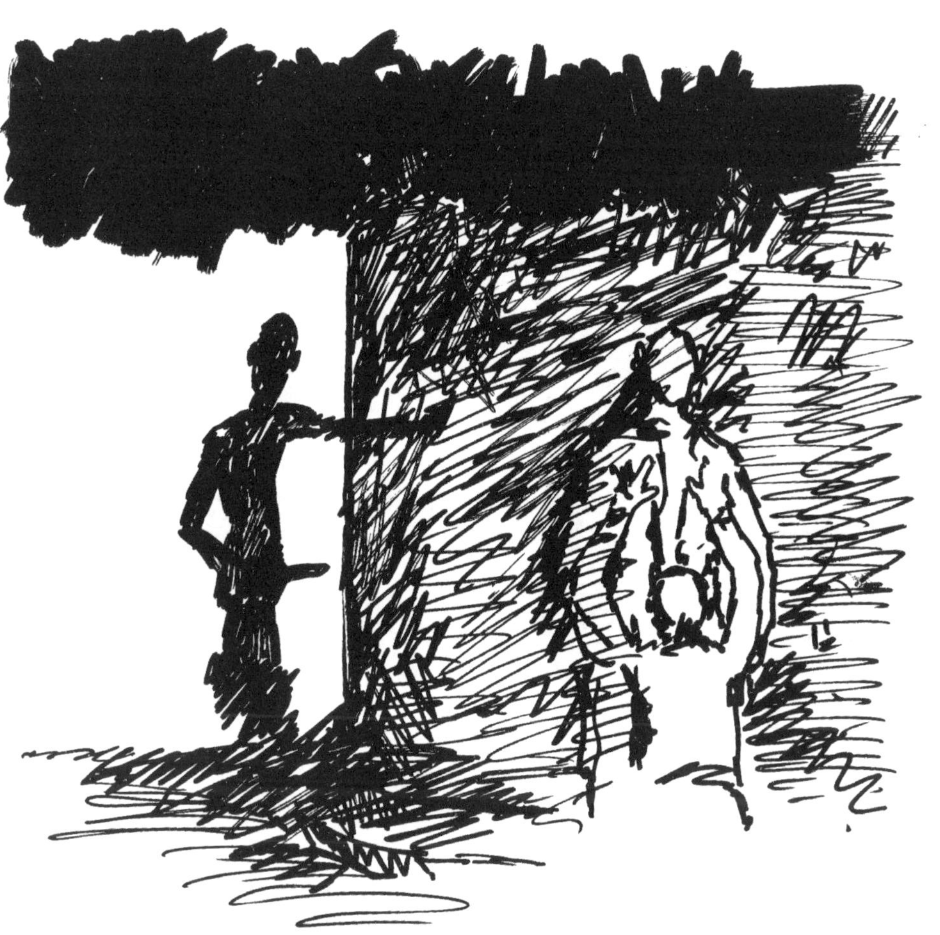

i saw this in a park on 2nd avenue one night. I wish my eyes were movie cameras so i could record scenes like this in movement.

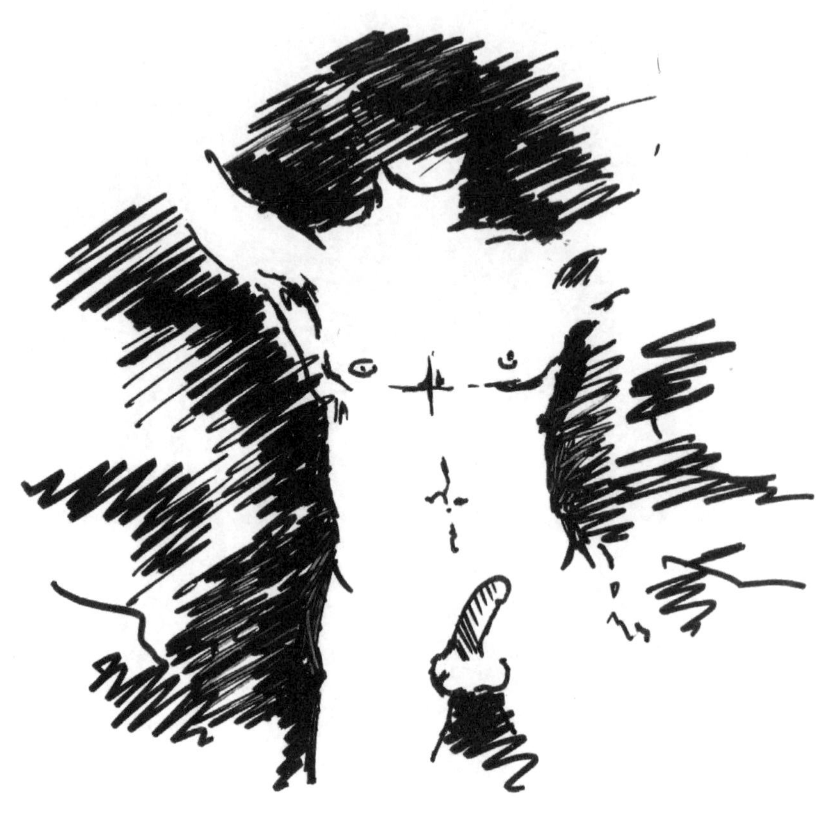

this is his body reaching up towards me
as I lay down on him. I was drunk.

is stirring this feeling inside me, signs of physical distress, the evening news, all the flags in the streets and the zombie population going about its daily routines. I just want to puke it all out like an intense projectile. I sidetrack myself by concentrating on the little lights at dusk; imagining one of them developing a puff of smoke in its engines and plummeting to the earth among the canyon streets. Any event would help. The nurse finally shows up and behind the curtains I hear the sounds of a body thumping, the sounds of cloth being rolled up, of water splashing and the covers being unfurled and tucked. Finally she leaves taking the smell of shit with her in a laundry cart. My friend wakes up and starts weeping; he's hallucinating that he can't find something that probably never existed. I understand the feeling just like I understand it when he sometimes screams that he hates healthy people. A senate group was in new york city recently collecting information on the extent of the epidemic and were told that in the next year and a half there will be thirty-three thousand homeless people with AIDS living in the streets and gutters of the city. A couple of people representing the policy of the city government assured the senators that these people were dying so fast from lack of health care that they were making room for the others coming up from behind; so there would be no visible increase of dying homeless on the streets. Oh I feel so sick. I feel like a human bomb tick tick tick.

7

I had an odd sleep last night. I felt like I was lying in a motel room for hours half awake or maybe I was just dreaming that I was half awake. In some part of my sleep I saw this fat little white worm, a grub-like thing that was no bigger than a quarter of an inch. When I leaned very close to it, my eye just centimeters above it, I could see every detail of the ridges of its flesh. It was a meat eater. The worm had latched onto something that looked like a goat fetus. It had large looping horns protruding from its head. The whole thing was white, fetal in appearance, its horns were translucent like fingernails. The grub was beginning to eat it and I pulled it off. It became very agitated and angry and tried to eat my fingers. I threw it onto the ground but there was yet another one and it was crawling toward some other fetal looking thing. I smacked it really hard. Picked it up and threw it down but my actions didn't kill it. My location was a wet dark hillside around dawn or dusk with a little light drifting over the landscape. Looking around I realized that the entire contents of a biology lab or pet shop had been dumped on the ground. Maybe I had stolen everything. There were big black tarantulas, all sorts of lizards, some small mammals and bugs and frogs and snakes. At some point a big black tarantula was crawling around, blue-black and the size of a catcher's mitt. It made a little jump like it had seized something. I looked closely and saw it was eating an extraordinarily beautiful monitor lizard, a baby one. The spider didn't scare me; my sense of anxiety came from mixing the species. They all seemed to have come from different countries and were now thrown accidently together by research or something. I pushed at the spider, picked it up and tried to unfasten its mandibles from the belly of the lizard. Someone else was with me; I handed them the spider and said, Take it somewhere else or put it in something until I figure out what I'm doing. The person threw the spider on the ground in a rough manner. I said, Don't do that, you'll kill it. If you drop a tarantula from a height higher than five inches its abdomen will burst.

8

Fevers. I wake up these mornings feeling wet like something from my soul, my memory is seeping out the back of my head onto the cloth of the pillows. I woke up earlier with intense nausea and headache. I turned on the television to try to get some focus outside my illness. Every station was filled with half-hour commercials disguised as talk shows in which low-grade tv actors and actresses talk about how to whiten your teeth or raise your investment earnings or shake the extra pounds from your bones. I am convinced I am from another planet. One station had a full closeup of a woman's face, middle-aged, saying, People talk about a sensation they've experienced when they are close to death in which their entire lives pass before their eyes. Well, you experience a similar moment when you are about to kill someone. You look at that person and see something in the moment before you kill him. You see his home, his family, his childhood, his hopes and beliefs, his sorrows and joys; all this passes before you in a flash. I didn't know what she was making these references for. The nausea comes back. I try a new position on the bed with some pillows and slip back into sleep. I'm walking through this city not really sure where or why. I've got to piss really bad and go down this staircase of a subway or a hotel. (Architecture grows around my moving body like stone vegetation.) I find this old bathroom, mostly metal stalls and shadows like the subway station toilets of my childhood. I could sense sex as soon as I walked in, the moist scent of it in the yellow light and wet tiles and concrete. I go into this stall and pull out my dick and start pissing into the toilet. A big section of the stall's divider is peeled away and I see this guy in his late teens early twenties jerking off watching me. When I finish I reach through the partition and feel his chest through his shirt. He zips up and comes around into my stall and closes the door and leans against it his hands on his thighs. I unzip his trousers and peel them down to his knees. I roll up his shirt so I can play with his belly. When his pants are down at his knees I notice a fairly large wound on one of his thighs, lots of scrapes and scratches on his body. The wound does something to me. I feel vaguely nauseous but he is sexy enough to dispel it. He pulls down his underwear and leans back again like he wants me to blow him. I crouch and slowly start licking under the base of his prick. The wound is close to my eye and I notice this series of red and green and yellow wires, miniature cables looping out of it. There are two chrome cables with sectioned ribs pushing under the sides of flesh. Then this blue glow coloring the air above the wound. I stop licking and look closer and see it is a miniature monitor, a tiny black and white television screen with an even tinier figure gesticulating from a podium in a vast room. There is the current president, smiling like a corpse in a vigilante movie, addressing the nation on a live controlled broadcast; the occasion is an enormous banquet in washington, a cannibal banquet attended by heads of state and the usual cronies; kirkpatrick and her biological warfare husband. The pope is seated next to buckley and his sidekick buchanan. Oliver north is part of the entertainment and he squats naked in a spotlight in the center of the ballroom floor. A small egg pops out of his ass and breaks in two on the floor. A tiny american flag tumbles out of the egg waving mechanically. The crowd breaks into wild applause as whitney houston steps forward to lead a rousing rendition of the star spangled banner. I wake up in a fever so delirious I am in a patriotic panic. Where, where the fuck at five in the morning could I run and buy a big american flag. My head hurts so bad I have to get out of bed and stand upright in order to ease the pressure. I go to the bathroom and finally throw up. I come back into the room, yank open the window and lean out above the dark empty streets and scream: THERE IS SOMETHING IN MY BLOOD AND IT'S TRYING TO FUCKING KILL ME.

9

I still fight the urge to puke. I've been fighting it all week. Whenever I witness signs of physical distress I have to fight the urge to bend over at the waist and empty out. It can be anything. The bum on the comer with festering sores on his face. It could be the moving skeleton I pass in the hall on the way in. Some guy with wasting syndrome and cmv blindness who is leaning precariously out his wheelchair in the unattended hallway searching in sightlessness for something he's lost. He's making braying sounds. What he's looking for is beneath the wheels of his chair. A tiny teddy bear with a collegiate outfit sewn to its body and a little flag glued to its paw. I pick it up and notice it has saliva and food matter stuck in its fur and I wonder if this is what civilization boils down to. I place it in the guy's hands and he squeals at me, his eyes a dull gray like the bellies of small fish. I have to resist that urge to puke. It's upsetting but I realize I'm only nauseated by my own mortality.

My friend on the bed is waking. The hospital gown has pulled up along his torso in the motions of sleep revealing a blobby looking penis and schools of cancer lesions twisting around his legs and abdomen. He opens his eyes too wide a couple of times and I hand him a bunch of flowers. I see double, he says. Twice as many flowers, I say.

10

Sometimes I come to hate people because they can't see where I am. I've gone empty, completely empty and all they see is the visual form; my arms and legs, my face, my height and posture, the sounds that come from my throat. But I'm fucking empty. The person I was just one year ago no longer exists; drifts spinning slowly into the ether somewhere way back there. I'm a xerox of my former self. I can't abstract my own dying any longer. I am a stranger to others and to myself and

I refuse to pretend that I am familiar or that I have history attached to my heels. I am glass, clear empty glass. I see the world spinning behind and through me. I see casualness and mundane effects of gesture made by constant populations. I look familiar but I am a complete stranger being mistaken for my former selves. I am a stranger and I am moving. I am moving on two legs soon to be on all fours. I am no longer animal vegetable or mineral. I am no longer made of circuits or disks. I am no longer coded and deciphered. I am all emptiness and futility. I am an empty stranger, a carbon copy of my form. I can no longer find what I'm looking for outside of myself. It doesn't exist out there. Maybe it's only in here, inside my head. But my head is glass and my eyes have stopped being cameras, the tape has run out and nobody's words can touch me. No gesture can touch me. I've been dropped into all this from another world and I can't speak your language any longer. See the signs I try to make with my hands and fingers. See the vague movements of my lips among the sheets. I'm a blank spot in a hectic civilization. I'm a dark smudge in the air that dissipates without notice. I feel like a window, maybe a broken window. I am a glass human. I am a glass human disappearing in rain. I am standing among all of you waving my invisible arms and hands. I am shouting my invisible words. I am getting so weary. I am growing tired. I am waving to you from here. I am crawling around looking for the aperture of complete and final emptiness. I am vibrating in isolation among you. I am screaming but it comes out like pieces of clear ice. I am signaling that the volume of all this is too high. I am waving. I am waving my hands. I am disappearing. I am disappearing but not fast enough.

DAVID WOJNAROWICZ was an accomplished artist, writer, and activist, born September 14, 1954. He came to prominence in New York in the 1980s, part of a cohort of East Village artists including Nan Goldin, Kiki Smith, Karen Finley and Peter Hujar. His work—from the graffiti that first brought him recognition in his teens to the photography and films produced before his AIDS-related death at the age of thirty-seven—center his experience on the margins of American society. His multi-media artworks and political advocacy were the focus of a Whitney retrospective, which named both as signs of his "radical possibility."

AMY SCHOLDER produces media that empowers underserved communities to tell their stories. She has served as an editor at City Lights Books, The Feminist Press, Verso, Seven Stories, Artspace Books, and HIGH RISK Books/Serpent's Tail. She produced the documentary feature films *Heightened Scrutiny* (2025), *My Name Is Andrea* (2023), and *Disclosure* (2020).

OCEAN VUONG is the author of the poetry collections *Time Is a Mother* (2022) and *Night Sky With Exit Wounds* (2016), winner of the 2017 T.S. Eliot Prize, and the novels *The Emperor of Gladness* (2025) and *On Earth We're Briefly Gorgeous* (2019). He serves as a professor in the MFA Program at New York University.

NIGHTBOAT BOOKS

Nightboat Books, a nonprofit organization, seeks to develop audiences for writers whose work resists convention and transcends boundaries. We publish books rich with poignancy, intelligence, and risk. Please visit nightboat.org to learn about our titles and how you can support our future publications.

Memories That Smell Like Gasoline was supported by Megan Adams, George Albon, Kazim Ali, Ava Aviva Avnisan, Jean C. Ballantyne, Star Black, Will Blythe, William Bruns, Cynthia Carr, Elisabeth Carruthers, V. Shannon Clyne, Theodore Cornwell, Katharine Crane, Moyra Davey, David Michael DiGregorio, Gisela Gamper, Richard Gerrig & Timothy Peterson, Photios Giovanis, Amanda Greenberger, Garth Greenwell, David Groff, Jonathan Groff, Roberto Erwin Gutierrez, Tom Healy, Parag Rajendra Khandhar, Shane Khosropour, Sue Landers, Katy Lederer, Shari Leinwand, Johanna Li, Elizabeth Madans, Ricardo Maldonado, Ethan Mitchell, Caren Motika, Elizabeth Motika, Achim Nowak, The Estate of Thomas W. Rauffenbart, Sarah Riggs, Asker Saeed, The Leslie Scalapino - O Books Fund, Amy Scholder, Mark Sexton, Thomas Shardlow, Benjamin Taylor, Avery Trufelman, Jerrie Whitfield & Richard Motika, Clay Williams, and the Collectors' Circle: David Bolger, Stephen Dull, and Will Palley.

We thank the above individuals for their generosity and commitment to the mission of Nightboat Books.

This book is made possible, in part, by grants from the New York City Department of Cultural Affairs in partnership with the City Council, and the New York State Council on the Arts Literature Program.

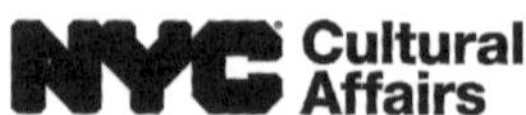

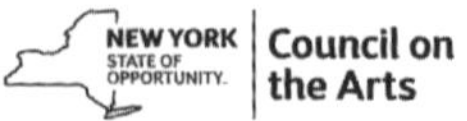